Hooray for Beekeeping!

A Bobbie Kalman Book
Crabtree Publishing Company

Hooray for Beekeeping!

A Bobbie Kalman Book

For Tom Stavraky and Lynda McCaig, you're the bee's knees!

Editor-in-Chief
Bobbie Kalman

Writing team
Bobbie Kalman
Allison Larin
Niki Walker

Text and photo research
Allison Larin

Managing editor
Lynda Hale

Editors
Niki Walker
Greg Nickles
Virginia Mainprize

Computer design
Lynda Hale
Campbell Creative Services
  (cover type)

Production coordinator
Hannelore Sotzek

Teacher Consultants from
Ontario Agri-Food Education

Special thanks to
Sandra Hawkins of Ontario Agri-Food Education; Ron Miksha;
Tom Stavraky; Pat Westlake of the Ontario Beekeepers' Association;
Danielle Gentile; Victoria Chuop; David-Anthony Turinek

Photographs
AGstockUSA/George Lepp: page 27
Bruce Arppe: title page, pages 5, 18
Marc Crabtree: page 31 (top)
Bobbie Kalman: pages 30, 31 (bottom)
Diane Payton Majumdar: page 14
Jeff March: page 10
Lynda McCaig: pages 16 (right), 20
Penny McCaig: front and back covers, pages 19, 24
Ontario Beekeepers' Association: page 22
Photo Researchers, Inc.: Scott Camazine: pages 11, 15;
  Nigel Cattlin: page 4
Allen Blake Sheldon: pages 13, 16 (left)
Dick Todd/Photo USA: pages 8, 28

Illustrations
Barbara Bedell: page 12
Cori Marvin: back cover art, border, pages 6, 7, 8, 9, 11, 14,
  17, 18, 21, 23, 29
Jeannette R. Julich: page 25

Crabtree Publishing Company

350 Fifth Avenue
Suite 3308
New York
N.Y. 10118

360 York Road, RR 4,
Niagara-on-the-Lake,
Ontario, Canada
L0S 1J0

73 Lime Walk
Headington
Oxford OX3 7AD
United Kingdom

Cataloging in Publication Data
Kalman, Bobbie
  Hooray for beekeeping!

(Hooray for farming!)
Includes index

ISBN 0-86505-654-4 (library bound)   ISBN 0-86505-668-4 (pbk.)
This book introduces bees and beekeeping, covering such aspects
as pollination, the making of honey, and beekeeping equipment
and practices.

1. Bee culture—Juvenile literature. 2. Honeybee—Juvenile literature.
3. Honey—Juvenile literature. [1. Bee culture. 2. Honeybee. 3. Bees.
4. Honey.] I. Title. II. Series: Kalman, Bobbie. Hooray for farming!

SF523.5.K35 1997   j638'.1   LC 97-31450
                                               CIP

The buzz on beekeeping

Bees and beekeepers

What do you do when you see a bee? You probably move away from it because you think it may sting you. Bees sometimes sting, but they also do many other things that are helpful to people.

Busy bees

Bees are very useful. They make honey and wax. They help plants grow. They are so useful that some people keep them on farms the way other farmers keep cows or sheep.

Why keep bees?

A bee farm is an **apiary**, and a bee farmer is called a **beekeeper**. Beekeepers raise bees and care for them. Some beekeepers sell the honey and wax made by bees. Others rent their bees to fruit and vegetables farmers. Bees help fruit and vegetable farmers grow large crops.

Hooray for bees and beekeepers!

The next time you see a bee, thank it for making honey. Shout "Hooray for bees!" When you next eat honey, shout "Hooray for beekeepers!" Beekeepers look after bees and get the honey for you to enjoy.

A bit about bees

Bees live in large groups called **colonies**. A colony of bees lives in a **hive**. The bees eat, raise young bees, and store extra food inside the hive. Three types of bees live in a colony: the queen bee, worker bees, and drones. The different types of bees have different jobs.

The queen bee

Each colony has one **queen bee**. She is the only female bee that can lay eggs. She is the mother of all the bees in the colony. The queen is also the leader.

Worker bees

Almost all the bees in a colony are **worker bees**. Worker bees are female bees that cannot lay eggs. Young worker bees are called **house bees**. They clean the hive, make honey, and care for the younger bees. Older worker bees are called **forager bees**. They gather food for the colony and defend the hive from enemies.

Drones

Drones are male bees. There are very few drones in a colony. A drone's job is to mate with the queen bee so that she can lay eggs.

From egg to adult bee

The queen bee lays all the eggs. The eggs take 21 days to become bees. During that time, they go through different stages from egg to adult. You can see the stages in these illustrations.

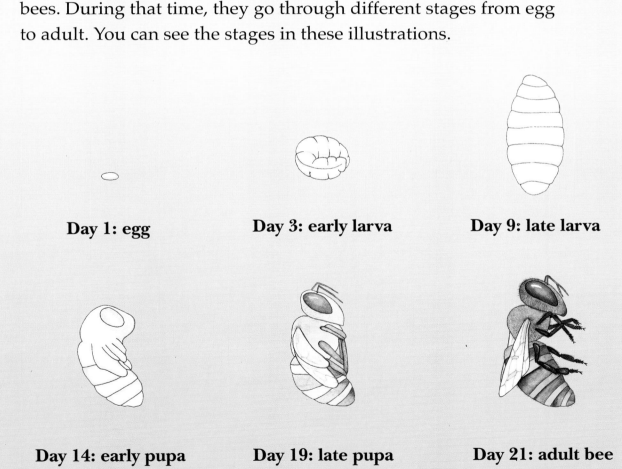

Day 1: egg

Day 3: early larva

Day 9: late larva

Day 14: early pupa

Day 19: late pupa

Day 21: adult bee

Why bees build combs

Bees build structures called **combs**. There are many combs in each beehive. Bees store honey and pollen in combs. The queen bee also lays eggs in them.

Each comb is made of thousands of **cells**. A cell is a small storage space. The cells are slanted slightly upward so that whatever the bees put inside them will not fall out.

Cells have six sides.

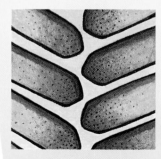

A side view shows how cells slant.

These bees are storing pollen and honey in the comb cells. The white cells on the left have been capped with wax.

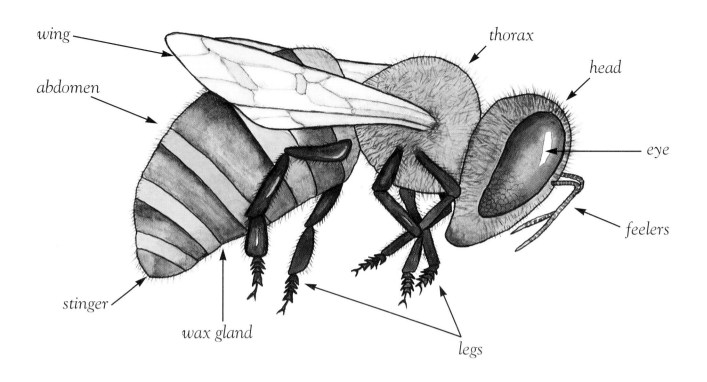

wing
abdomen
stinger
wax gland
thorax
head
eye
feelers
legs

Building a comb

Combs are made from wax. To build their combs, bees first have to make wax inside their body. Worker bees have a special body part called a **wax gland**. The wax gland is on their abdomen.

Spit and shape

The wax comes out of the gland as a liquid. It hardens quickly. A bee puts the hard wax into her mouth and chews it to make it soft. Then she spits out the wax and shapes it into a comb cell.

Making honey

Bees do not make honey for money. They make honey to feed themselves. To make honey, forager bees collect **nectar**, a sweet liquid found in flowers. The forager bee sticks out her long tongue and sucks up the nectar. She stores the nectar in a special stomach called the **honey stomach**.

Turning nectar into honey

When the forager bee's honey stomach is full, she flies back to the hive. She passes the nectar to a house bee, who swallows it. In the house bee's honey stomach, chemicals called **enzymes** are added to the nectar.

The nectar slowly turns into a drop of honey, which the house bee puts into a comb cell. She fans the honey with her wings to dry up any extra water. When the cell is full of honey, the bee closes it with a cap of wax. The bee in the picture is filling a comb cell with honey.

We get the leftovers

Bees make a lot more honey than they need. The beekeeper takes the extra honey to sell. He or she must be careful not to take too much, or the bees will starve.

How bees pollinate

Pollination is the most important job that bees do in nature. It is also a big help to farmers. Many plants cannot make fruits and vegetables without pollination. Apples, watermelons, plums, pears, blueberries, cherries, and cucumbers all grow on plants that need to be pollinated.

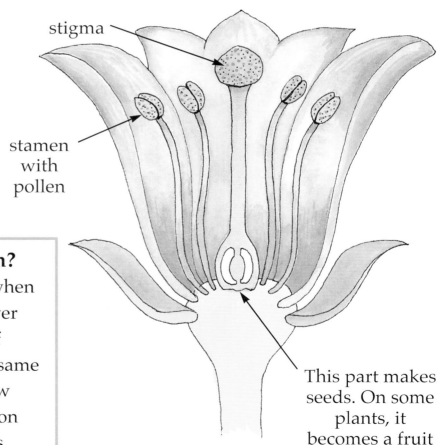

stigma

stamen
with
pollen

This part makes seeds. On some plants, it becomes a fruit or vegetable.

What is pollination?
Pollination happens when the **pollen** of one flower lands on the stigma of another flower of the same kind. Pollen is a yellow powder that is found on the stamens of flowers.

Bees pollinate by accident

As a bee crawls around a flower to gather food, her legs and body get covered with pollen. When she lands on another flower, pollen rubs off her body and onto the flower's stigma. The bee below is covered with pollen. She will pollinate many flowers in a day.

Bees at work

When it is sunny and warm, forager bees spend the day collecting nectar and pollen from flowers. They start when the sun comes up and spend the day going from flower to flower. When they find pollen, bees let other bees know where it is by doing special dances called the wagtail dance and round dance.

The round dance

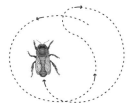

This dance tells how far away the food is.

The wagtail dance

This dance shows the direction of the food.

Pollen baskets

Forager bees collect pollen to feed to the young bees in the hive. Each bee has a pollen basket on her hind legs in which she stores pollen. She collects pollen on her body, moistens it with nectar, and then scrapes it into her pollen baskets with her legs.

The bee returns to the hive when her pollen baskets are full of pollen and her honey stomach is full of nectar.

Bees always come home

Bees belong to one colony, and the queen bee is their leader. A beekeeper does not worry that the bees will leave for good. Bees always return to their hive.

Back at the hive

While forager bees gather food, house bees are busy storing pollen in cells, making honey, and cleaning the hive. They feed and clean the other bees. In the picture above, some bees are storing food in cells, and others are cleaning empty cells.

What is an apiary hive?

In nature, bees make their own hives. At an apiary, the beekeeper provides the bees with a hive. An apiary hive looks very different from the kind bees build for themselves. The apiary hive opens easily so that the beekeeper can check the bees and reach the wax and honey.

(below) In nature, bees often build their hives inside dead trees.

(right) These beekeepers are looking at what is happening inside their apiary hives. The hives are easy to open and check.

Boxes and frames

The hive is made up of several boxes. Each box is filled with frames. The bees make their combs on the frames. The hive has two covers to keep out rain, snow, dirt, and animals.

covers

The worker bees store honey in the **honey supers**.

The **queen excluder** keeps the queen bee in the broodchamber and stops her from laying eggs in the honey supers.

frames

The **broodchamber** is the box in which the queen bee lives and lays eggs. House bees raise young bees in the broodchamber.

The **hive stand** keeps the hive off the ground so that it does not get too cold or wet.

17

Beekeeping tools

Beekeepers need special tools to help them work with the bees and hives. They also wear special clothes that protect them from bee stings.

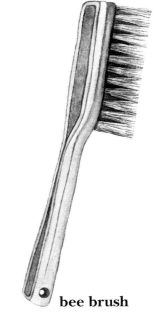

bee brush

Hive equipment

The **hive tool** is used to pull apart the sticky frames. The **smoker** sprays light smoke into the hives. Smoke calms the bees so they will not sting. The **bee brush** is used to brush bees off the frames before they are taken from the hive.

hive tool

smoker

A beekeeper sprays smoke into a hive to calm the bees before taking their combs.

Clothing

To protect themselves from bee stings, beekeepers wear gloves, boots, and coveralls. They also wear a broad-rimmed hat with a veil that keeps bees from landing on their face or in their hair, mouth, or ears. The beekeepers in the picture are well protected. Every part of their body is covered so bees cannot sting them.

Wearing white

Bees can see dark colors better than they can see light colors or white. When they become angry, they look for someone or something to sting. A dark-colored outfit shows the bees exactly where to sting. A light-colored or white outfit "hides" the beekeeper from the bees so that they do not have a target to sting.

Collecting honey

Beekeepers collect honey and wax in
August. Some beekeepers package the
honey and wax themselves and sell them
at a local market. Others sell the honey
and wax to factories, which then sell
honey and wax products to stores.

Checking the hives

In the summer, the hives are checked every two weeks. When the combs are full of honey, the beekeeper removes them from the hive. By the end of August, no more honey can be taken. The bees must begin storing it for the coming winter.

Slicing off the caps

The beekeeper uses a thin knife to slice off the tiny wax caps that seal the comb cells. He or she then places the combs in an **extractor** like this one.

Spinning the combs

An extractor is a big cylinder that spins the combs around quickly. It works in the same way as the spin cycle on a washing machine. The force of spinning pulls the honey out of the combs, just as water is pulled out of clothes as they spin in a washing machine.

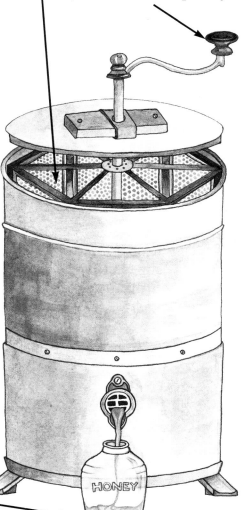

The beekeeper places frames of comb on the sides of the extractor.

The beekeeper turns the handle to spin the frames around quickly.

The honey drips down to the bottom of the cylinder, where the beekeeper collects it.

21

How honey is sold

At a grocery store you can find different kinds of honey: **comb**, **liquid**, and **creamed** honey. Comb honey is sold in pieces of comb that have been cut apart and packaged.

Liquid and creamed honey are sold in jars and bottles. Liquid honey is gold-colored, clear, and runny. Creamed honey is light yellow or white and very thick.

22

How wax is used

After beekeepers remove the honey from the wax combs, they put them in a **wax melter** and place it in sunlight. The sun melts the wax, and it becomes a liquid. The hot liquid wax runs down through a filter that removes any dirt. The filtered wax drips into a container.

As the wax cools, it hardens into a solid block. The beekeeper sells the blocks of wax to factories, where the wax is used to make many kinds of products.

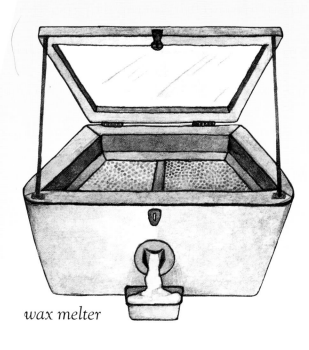

wax melter

People use beeswax to make candles, crayons, lipstick, lotions, and polishes for cars, furniture, and shoes.

23

Keeping bees healthy and safe

Beekeepers are always busy caring for and checking their bees. If bees are sick, beekeepers give them medicine. If the bees do not have enough honey to eat in winter, the beekeeper feeds them sugar syrup. Beekeepers also try to keep away insects and animals that eat bees or destroy hives.

Yellow jackets feed bees to their young.

Insects that eat bees

Ants and yellow-jacket wasps eat bees. Yellow jackets wait until bees are returning to the hive with full pollen baskets. When their legs are loaded with pollen, bees fly more slowly and are easy to catch.

Ants crawl inside hives to eat the bees.

Warm hives

Before winter arrives, the bee-keeper wraps the hives in tar paper or burlap. The cover protects the bees from cold winds and snow.

Furry enemies

Bears love honey. A bear will destroy a beehive and kill many bees in order to get honey. They do not mind being stung by hundreds of bees!

Skunks don't want honey. They eat the bees. They often scratch on the front of a beehive at night to wake up the bees. When the worker bees come out to see what is happening, the skunk eats them.

Skunks use their long, tough tongues to lick up bees as they fly out of the hive.

On the road

To earn extra money, beekeepers move their hives to fruit farms so the bees can pollinate the plants. The beekeepers are paid by the farmer, and they also sell the bees' honey.

Moving the bees

Some beekeepers travel across the country with their bees. They are called **migratory beekeepers**. During the summer, they stay in the north, where their bees make honey and pollinate crops. When the weather cools in autumn, the beekeepers load their beehives and bees onto big trucks.

Heading south for the winter

Migratory beekeepers drive to Florida and California, where it is warm all year. The bees pollinate the orange, lemon, and grapefruit trees that grow fruit during the winter.

No sleep for these bees!

Migratory beekeeping is becoming popular. Beekeepers earn money year-round because their bees do not spend the winter sleeping.

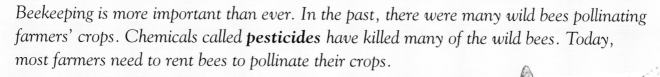

Beekeeping is more important than ever. In the past, there were many wild bees pollinating farmers' crops. Chemicals called **pesticides** have killed many of the wild bees. Today, most farmers need to rent bees to pollinate their crops.

27

Why do bees sting?

Bees sting people and animals to protect their queen bee and their hive. Only female bees have stingers.

For most people, a bee sting hurts only for a few minutes. It turns red and swells. The area around the sting is red and itchy for a few days. Some people, however, get very sick from a bee sting. This picture shows a bee stinging a person. OUCH!

What happens when you get stung?

When a bee stings you, it pushes its stinger into your skin. Its pumper pumps venom into you. The bee flies away, but its stinger, pumper, and venom sac stay in your skin. The pumper continues to pump venom. After stinging, the bee dies.

Parts of the stinger

The **shaft** of the stinger has **barbs** on it. Barbs make it difficult to pull out the stinger.

The **venom sac** holds the venom. Venom is a mild poison that makes the sting sore, red, and itchy.

The **pumper** is a muscle that pumps venom into a victim.

> **Warning:**
> If you get stung by a bee, tell an adult right away! You may have an allergy to bee stings.

Honey delights

Do you like honey? Some people eat honey on toast or in a sandwich. Some bake with honey instead of sugar. Honey is natural and healthier for you than white sugar. Here are two recipes that use honey. Using honey will make your hands feel sticky. Ask an adult to help you make these treats.

Sweet-and-Sticky Apple Sandwiches

1 apple sliced into thin pieces
2 slices of bread
peanut butter
honey

Spread peanut butter and a layer of honey on one piece of bread. Place the apple slices on top and cover with the second piece of bread. Take a big bite and enjoy!

A little tip:
Always measure your honey in a measuring cup or spoon that has been coated with butter. This coating will help the honey flow easily from the cup or spoon.

Honey Circles

1 cup (250 ml) of melted butter
1 cup (250 ml) of honey
2 cups (500 ml) of coarsely
   ground sunflower seeds
1 tsp (5 ml) of vanilla
2$\frac{1}{2}$ cups (625 ml) of
   whole-wheat pastry flour

Combine the butter, honey, and vanilla in a bowl. Stir in the flour and sunflower seeds. Mix well. With both hands, roll the dough into small balls. Place the balls on a greased cookie sheet and flatten them with a fork. Bake at 350° F (175° C) for 15 minutes. Makes 30 cookies.

Beekeeping words

apiary A bee farm

comb cell A small compartment or storage area where bees store honey or pollen

colony A large group of bees that lives together

drone A male bee

forager bee A bee that collects pollen and brings it to the hive

hive A home for bees

honey comb A wax structure built by bees, made up of six-sided cells

house bee A bee that feeds and cleans the queen, drones, and young bees

nectar A sweet liquid that is found in many flowers

pollen A yellow powdery substance found inside flowers

pollen baskets Little pouches on the side of a bee's legs used for carrying pollen

pollinate To carry pollen from one flower to another so that seeds can be made

queen bee A female bee that lays all the eggs in a hive. Only one queen bee lives in a hive.

worker bee A forager or house bee; worker bees gather food and make honey

Index

1 2 3 4 5 6 7 8 9 0 Printed in the U.S.A. 6 5 4 3 2 1 0 9 8 7